Three Bricks Shy of a Load

A collection of true stories about ordinary people doing really dumb stuff!

Peter Taylor

Fitzhenry & Whiteside

**Special thanks to those editors the world over who insist that these
stories are funny enough, and important enough to include in our radio
and television newscasts, and in our newspapers every day of the year.**

Fitzhenry and Whiteside Limited
195 Allstate Parkway
Markham, Ontario L3R 4T8

In the United States:
121 Harvard Avenue, Suite 2
Allston, Massachusetts 02134

www.fitzhenry.ca   godwit@fitzhenry.ca

Fitzhenry & Whiteside acknowledges with thanks the Canada Council
for the Arts, the Government of Canada through its Book Publishing
Industry Development Program, and the Ontario Arts Council for their
support of our publishing program.

10 9 8 7 6 5 4 3

National Library of Canada Cataloguing in Publication Data

Taylor, Peter
Three bricks shy of a load : a collection of true stories about
ordinary people doing really dumb stuff

ISBN 1-55041-624-3

1. Canadian wit and humor (English) I. Title.

PN6231.H763T388 2001   C818'.5402   C2001-903160-2

Design and typesetting: Kinetics Design & Illustration
Cover image courtesy of Hulton Archive / Getty Images
Printed and bound in Canada

Introction

Aman and a woman walk into a bar. The guy's had a really rough day at the office and wants to get it off his chest. But first, the woman has a funny story to tell, one she read in the paper that morning, a true story about a hunter who mistook another hunter for a turkey ... *a turkey, would you believe it?*

And they both laugh!

The story about the turkey reminds the bartender about something he read last week, and the bartender's story reminds the man who had the rough day about another story he read somewhere else, and before you know it, all three are laughing uproariously, and the fellow who had the bad day at the office has forgotten about it completely.

"Did you see that story about the guy in Toronto trying to steal a car and he's never driven a standard shift before so he's still there trying to get it moving when the cops show up and take him away?"

"Did you hear the one about that gal whose boyfriend they found all wrapped up in a duffel bag, in the hold of a Greyhound Bus! She couldn't afford the fare for two so she stuffed him in a bag under the bus."

Walk into any bar, saloon, or cocktail lounge at the end of the day and just as sure as God invented Monday Night Football, chocolate, dry martinis, waterproof mascara, and the six-pack – there's two things you'll hear.

You'll hear the sound of the weight of the world as it slips off the shoulders of men and women from the workaday world and lands on the floor.

And you'll hear weird stories.
Funny stories.

True stories about ordinary people who — for one brief moment — seem to have walked straight through the fun-house looking glass and taken upon themselves the thankless task of making the rest of us look good.

"Did you see that story about that woman in England who's suing her company, suing her boss for promoting her?"

"Did you hear about that fellow down in Tennessee who's girlfriend left him and now he's trying to get permission to marry his car?"

And the bartenders call the regulars by name as the drinks get mixed and the beer gets poured, and the bar talk bounces back and forth across the room.

Welcome to Happy Hour!

Having spent several happy hours in several bars throughout the United States and Canada over the past 40 years (and on occasion, on vacation in France and Spain), I am always amazed at the universality of schadenfreude.

I am also amazed at the speed with which these stories travel — one minute in a newspaper, tossed off in a radio or television newscast — the next, like a twister through a trailer park, ricocheting barstool to barstool around the world and back again.

In Madrid, a man accused of robbing a cab driver is temporarily acquitted when he convinces a judge that on the night in question he was picking pockets in another town.

In Montreal, a bride heads to divorce court after knocking out her husband at their wedding reception.

In Edmonton, a man pretending to be an undercover cop attempts to negotiate a fee-for-sex with a lady hooker who really is an undercover cop.

In Tehran, a guy gets a sex change operation then wants it reversed because he doesn't like being a woman.

The joy we take in the pratfalls of others achieves no bounds or boundaries.

Who are these people?

Where do they come from?

Or does it matter that we know, or even dare to care beyond the fact that it is they, not us, who are out there slipping on banana peels and forgetting to duck when the cream-filled pies are tossed their way.

Like the man, the lady, and the bartender at the beginning of this introduction, we laugh:

"Not the sharpest knife in the drawer," we chuckle, hearing the story about the man in Paris who is hauled off to hospital after trying to extinguish the eternal flame with his backside.

"The light was on, but no one was home," we tell each other.

"In need of a little mental flossing, perhaps," we say, or "Three bricks shy of a load."

And like the people in the following stories who for one brief moment have taken up the task of making the rest of us look good, we get a moment of our own in which to shine a little brighter, and feel a whole lot smarter, smugger, and safer ... at least for now.

Three Bricks
Shy of a
Load

Mornin' George, 'night George, Mornin' George, 'night George...

NEW YORK

EXECUTIVES at a mid-town publishing company say they are perplexed that one of their employees sat dead at his desk for five days before anyone noticed.

Medical examiners say the employee apparently died of a heart attack in the middle of the open-concept office he shared with 20 other workers at the firm. A post mortem examination indicates that the 51-year-old probably died quietly on a Monday, but his death went unnoticed until Saturday morning when a janitor stopped to ask him why he was working on the weekend.

A spokesperson for the publishing company described the employee as "the first guy in each morning, and the last guy to leave at night." He said the man was always absorbed in his work and kept pretty much to himself, which might explain why no one noticed that he was dead. He had been with the firm for 30 years.

Ironically, investigators say the man was proof-reading the manuscript of a medical textbook when he died.

OKAY THEN, DON'T EVERYBODY MOVE

DRESDEN, GERMANY

A would-be bank robber missed out on his chance to shout "DON'T ANYBODY MOVE" when he burst into an empty bank lobby only to be told by a workman that the bank he wanted to rob moved to a new location several days earlier.

Workmen readying the premises for the new tenants told police that the man entered the building wearing a mask and carrying a gun.

"He didn't believe us at first," said one carpenter. "We had to tell him several times that the bank was gone."

Police say the confused crook shook his firearm and swore at the workmen before fleeing the building.

Darn, We Seem to be Lost. Pass Me That Map, Honey. Just Kidding!

PHILADELPHIA

POLICE say the man they rescued from a portable toilet at a nearby campsite was after the car keys he had just lost down, "you-know-where."

The fellow, authorities say, compounded his problem tenfold when, instead of seeking help, he attempted to retrieve his keys single-handedly.

"It's a guy thing, I guess," one officer remarked on the kind of stubbornness that led to the man's predicament.

The unidentified man told police that after making sure no one was around, he removed his socks, shoes and pants and was attempting to lower himself into the lower chamber when he became stuck.

Fortunately, his cries for help were heard by campers who called police.

Witnesses say it took an emergency crew about 45 minutes to free the man who was stuck up to his hips in the waste compartment. Rescuers were forced to destroy much of the toilet getting him out.

Police say the man was treated for cuts and bruises at a nearby hospital where doctors also had to remove the toilet seat — which had become wedged around his torso like a Hula-Hoop.

Trigger Man Fingered by Thumb at Scene of Shooting

FORT LAUDERDALE, FLORIDA

POLICE say that while fingerprints left at the scene of a crime are a great help when it comes to solving murders, they're nothing compared to the real thing.

When three armed bandits burst into an auto body shop and threatened the owner, his wife and a customer at gunpoint, the owner decided to fight back.

According to police there was a scuffle which resulted in one of the bandit's thumbs being bitten clean off.

Combing the crime scene for evidence, police say they found the thumb among bullet casings on the floor of the shop.

Fingerprints from the thumb were quickly identified as those of a man already being sought on other charges.

In addition to his (thumb) prints, police now had another clue in their search to bring the bandit to justice — the man they were looking for had only one thumb.

Oh Yeah, Well I'm Not Even From Edmonton, So There

EDMONTON

A 35-year-old Edmonton man was arrested for attempting to get free sex by posing as a police officer in the city's red light district.

Unfortunately for the make-believe policeman, the lady he propositioned was the real McCoy — an undercover policewoman posing as a prostitute.

Police say the man struck up a conversation with the lady cop, and even flashed fake police ID while suggesting that he would let her go if she would consider providing her services free of charge — or at least at rock-bottom prices.

It was at this point that the undercover officer signaled her backup, and two detectives arrested the cheapskate imposter right on the spot.

Look, Up There in The Sky…It's a Log, It's a Tree, It's A Telephone Pole

PICTON, ONTARIO

A 23-year-old vandal was knocked down and pinned to the ground in a citizen's arrest which police say was executed by one very public-spirited citizen and one very solid telephone pole.

"Talk about your dynamic duos," says a witness to the capture.

Police say this mindless lout had been attempting to kick in the windows of a car on the town's main street, when a man driving by leapt from his vehicle and confronted him.

As the vandal fled the scene, the public-spirited citizen gave chase.

Police say the pursuit ended when the suspect looked back over his shoulder to see if his pursuer was gaining ground.

"That's when the telephone pole stepped in and this guy ran into it, smack, head first," said one officer.

By the time police arrived the 20-year-old do-gooder had the suspect pinned to the ground.

We Knew They'd Want a Beer, and We Also Knew They Had No Deodorant

SACKVILLE, NEW BRUNSWICK

As any prison warden knows, you live with a guy for a year or two, and you get to know his habits.

That being the case, it didn't take guards at nearby Dorchester Penitentiary very long to track down two prisoners who managed to slip out of the prison grounds by stowing away on a garbage truck.

Jail officials say the escapees were picked up later the same day, belly-up to the bar of a local tavern.

"It's the first pub you come to driving south from the pen," said a spokesperson for the warden's office. "So it's the first place we looked."

U.S. Soldier Fined for Drunken Rowdiness Signs Contract to Endorse Canadian Beer

TORONTO

CANADIANS love to brag about their beer, especially when it's placed head-to-head with that watery stuff sold south of the 49th parallel.

Like moose on the highway, Mounties, Margaret Atwood and back bacon, our beer makes the short list of those things that make us the rugged individuals of the Great North Woods we call home.

Obviously familiar with our pride in such things, a U.S. soldier arrested near Toronto for drunken rowdiness, resisting arrest, and insulting police officers, threw himself on the mercy of the Canuck court with crossed fingers and a bit of cross border flattery.

Pleading guilty to the charges, Jason Dalgai blamed his uncharacteristic behavior on that particularly powerful Canadian beer. The soldier, from Flagstaff, Arizona, opined that our extra strong and extra tasty brewskis had made him behave like a durned fool.

Aw shucks! The judge fined him anyway, in Canadian dollars.

And On The Dock, as Céline Dion Belted Out "My Heart Will Go On," I Thought I'd Cry

VAN BUREN, ARKANSAS

WHEN the engine caught fire and the fishing trawler, *Dos Amigos II*, ran aground, the two amigos on board quickly grabbed a flare gun, a fistful of flares, and abandoned ship.

Problem was, they were about nine metres from shore and standing in less than one metre of water.

"There they were, up to their waists in water, shooting off flares," said a local fisherman who helped rescue the two.

Police say the anything-but-seaworthy duo had been doing a "fair amount of drinking" when they decided to "borrow" the 13-metre trawler tied up at a nearby dock.

They had barely set sail when they ran aground.

I've Just Washed My Truck and I Can't Do a Thing With It

GREAT FALLS, MONTANA

CASCADE County Sheriff John Strandell is never quite sure which deserves the bigger fine — speeding, or the feeble excuses people trot out when they are nabbed for stupidity on the highways that crisscross this great nation.

Take the 28-year-old who, in one afternoon, was cited for reckless driving, charged with zipping through a 45 mph zone at 104 mph, and was finally inducted into that legion of story-telling motorists who are as quick with a story as they are with getting from A to B.

Says Sheriff Strandell, this particular piece of work, when stopped by a highway patrolman, explained that he had just finished washing his truck — and was simply trying to dry it off.

Okay, You Be Dead Ken, and I'll Be Dead Barbie, and This Can Be Dead Barbie's Friend Angel ...

SHELBY, MICHIGAN

THE decorations may have spruced up the yard and kept her children happy, but as far as police are concerned, a 30-year-old local woman is as guilty of grave robbing as she would be if she had pulled the coffins right out of the ground.

Officers investigating the mysterious thefts say that ceramic bunnies, vases, shepherds' staffs and musical angels began disappearing from local graveyards at least two years ago.

When approached, the suspect told police officers that the house she was renting was so rundown that she decided to spruce it up with flowers and lawn art from a nearby cemetery.

"It made the kids so happy," she told one officer, "that I started bringing home a new piece every time I went downtown."

What Part of %#*X!! %$%##@ **!!%! Don't You Understand!

VANCOUVER, WASHINGTON

GIVING it one last shot, a love-struck bachelor brandished an engagement ring and proposed to the victim of his obsession — during his trial for stalking her, burglarizing her apartment, and attempted kidnapping.

"Marry me," he shouted, as the poor woman bolted from her chair on the witness stand and ran from the courtroom.

"You mean everything to me," the besotted bozo hollered as officers of the court wrestled him into submission with handcuffs and shackles.

The man had been acting as his own lawyer when he asked to see the diamond and amethyst engagement ring that had earlier been entered into evidence.

The judge said he would not have allowed the obsessed man to question his victim if he had known the man was going to propose.

Hey!
I Was Just Thinking About You!

BERLIN

A SCIENTIFIC survey suggests that our hatred of cell phones may very well decrease in direct proportion to the intensity of our disinterest in the activity that the ringing of that infernal gadget interrupts.

Well, in Germany anyway.

It seems more Germans turn off their cell phones in movie theatres and restaurants than during sex.

Of 621 people surveyed, some 58 percent told pollsters that they always switched off their cell phones at the movies, while 46 percent said they shut off their "Handys" (as cell phones are called in Germany) in bars and restaurants.

By comparison, only 45 percent told the popular lifestyle magazine, *Focus*, that they shut their phones off during sex.

Other Than That, Mrs. Lincoln, Did You Enjoy The Play?

WINNIPEG

WHILE saying that such bureaucratic blunders are extremely rare, a Winnipeg hospital administrator was forced to apologize for a letter sent from the hospital to a dead man — asking how his stay in the hospital was.

Needless to say, the family of the deceased was not amused.

In a similar foul-up in London, Ontario, a spokesman for the province's health insurance plan admits that someone in his department informed an 81-year-old London area woman that she was dead.

Not only was she dead, the letter informed her, but if she persisted in using her health card, she would be charged with fraud.

If We Told Him Once, We Told Him a Dozen Times, Don't Believe Everything You Read

HALIFAX

SHE was everything the advertisement said she was — tall, blonde and lonely (except for the two guys waiting in the motel room where she suggested they go after dinner).

The victim — an out-of-town businessman — told police he met the young lady through a newspaper advertisement, wined her and dined her, and was thrilled to learn that she was staying in a motel on the edge of town. But not for long.

At the motel, the man was accosted and robbed by two goons who police believe were the woman's accomplices.

The victim suffered minor bruises, but did not require medical attention.

He did, however, need a new wallet, a new pair of trousers and a new pair of shoes.

Said one of the investigating officers, "It's hard to believe that in the year 2001 men still believe that sweet young women can be found in the want ads."

Put Down That Gun and Come Out With Your Drumsticks in the Air

MARTINSVILLE, VIRGINIA

IN what may be the saddest case of mistaken identity on record, two hunters ended up in hospital when one shot the other after mistaking him for a turkey, thereby prompting the other hunter to shoot back.

According to state wildlife officials, Danny Lea and Ray Durham were hunting separately when Lea spotted what he thought was a trophy gobbler. He hoisted his shotgun, and blasted Durham in the head and torso.

In what many might describe as a classic NRA response, Durham (whose friends say looks nothing like a turkey) fired back, a single shot that peppered pellets into Lea's back and shoulders.

Both men were treated at nearby Memorial Hospital and released, proving once again that guns don't kill turkeys ... or something like that.

Who Let The Dogs Out Narc, Narc, Narc, Narc Who Let The Dogs Out

MISSOULA, MONTANA

A pair of hard-luck Missoula gardeners had no idea that when they put the dog out, that same dog would turn them in.

But, according to local media reports, this is exactly what happened.

The pup, a black Labrador left outdoors longer than most sociable animals should, had been tied to an outdoor tap that soon gave way under the weight of his tugging.

Well, as Loudon Wainwright III might put it, before you know it, you got your broken tap, your flooded basement, and your landlord needing to get into the house to shut down the water main. And there in the house — according to the police who were called by the landlord — was the niftiest little indoor marijuana garden you ever did see.

A total of 21 plants, an unspecified amount of harvested marijuana, lights, scales, and other paraphernalia were seized.

A 23-year-old man and his 22-year-old girlfriend were arrested on various drug charges, including possession and production of dangerous drugs.

No word yet on whether the Lab will be rewarded for his bite on crime.

LOOK! Up in the Sky! It's a Bird... Yep, It's The Bird Alright

WINNIPEG

A local woman sued her doctor claiming an operation he performed on her hand left her with a permanent "road rage salute."

Her lawsuit claims that the doctor did not warn her of the risks of surgery nor did he offer any non-surgical alternatives.

Prior to the operation, the woman claimed her finger would occasionally "lock" into the unfortunate and embarrassing position.

Since the operation, she's "giving the finger" to people wherever she goes.

The lawsuit further alleges that the ongoing stress has given the woman angina, which has left her nervous about exploring further surgery.

When The Moon Hits Your Eye, Like the Fourth of July... THAT'S LASAGNA!

KANSAS CITY, MISSOURI

JIM Duddy admits it's a stretch, but says he'll never celebrate Independence Day again without thinking about good old fashioned Italian lasagna.

According to Duddy, Kansas City's Assistant Fire Marshall, it was just a few short hours after midnight on the Fourth of July when America's national holiday and that classic Italian dish became indelibly intertwined in his memory forever.

At approximately 3 a.m., in fact, a 28-year-old man who had been doing more than a little celebrating got a great big craving for a feed of lasagna. He turned on his oven and the resulting explosion blew his kitchen half way from Kansas City to Calabria.

The blast, according to the fire marshal's office, blew the kitchen apart, sending the entire oven right through one wall and knocking the other three walls to bits.

Seems that earlier in the evening neighbours complained about fireworks and noise from a nearby party and called police. Hearing that the law was on its way, one of the homeowner's buddies hid a stash of fireworks in the oven, and simply forgot to mention it.

WHAT WE HAVE HERE IS A FAILURE TO FIT BETWEEN THE BARS

CAPE TOWN, SOUTH AFRICA

HE might have been the brains behind one of the area's largest prison breaks, but prison officials say that when it came time for the actual escape, a 27-year-old Cape Town bartender just didn't have the stomach for it.

Reconstructing the breakout, a spokesman says it appears that car jacks smuggled into the penal institution at Malmesbury were used to force the bars apart, allowing seven men to scamper free.

Despite the car jacks, however, Fred Arkvijk, the man credited with masterminding the escape, stayed behind when his beer belly became wedged in the bars of his cell.

"I guess it's Fred's destiny to stay behind bars," commented one of his jailers.

"A bit more bread and water obviously wouldn't hurt him either," said another.

And During My Next Hold Up I Am Going to Flee the Scene After Shooting Myself in the Foot

TORONTO

ACCORDING to a Toronto police constable, a 20-year-old Toronto man charged with robbery and possession of an imitation firearm is simply "too stupid" to live a life of crime and should quickly find himself something else to do.

In one attempted robbery, a shop clerk simply ran out the back door of the shop when the young man announced his criminal intentions.

Faced with that sort of cooperation, the hapless lout could do little more than run out the front door and down the street.

In another attempt, the fellow actually got away with several hundred dollars, but drove his van off the road and into a ditch during his getaway. He was arrested at the scene of the accident.

"How many different ways can you spell stupid?" asked Constable Jerry Robertson. "This guy shouldn't bother with this kind of work at all."

Okay, That Was Just a Practice Shot, Now Here We Go For Real This Time

ARJAY, KENTUCKY

A 47-year-old ended up in hospital after sitting a beer car on the top of his head and asking his best buddy to shoot it off.

"I don't think there was an argument or anything. These guys are best friends," a police officer explained.

"The one that got shot just put the beer can on top of his head and told his pal to shoot it off. Unfortunately he missed the can and hit his head."

Police say that following the incident the shooter fled the scene and hid from police for about three hours before turning himself in.

As they say in some circles, "alcohol was involved."

Perhaps If He'd Asked Her While She Was in the Middle of Dinner…

MONTREAL

THE young telemarketer said the man asked about her sexual habits.

Then, she said, he asked her about a kiss.

Finally, the silver-tongued devil asked her about a buttock massage.

No, it didn't take place over the telephone, but in person, and in the office where they both worked.

And when the young lady in question said "no" to all of the above, the man in question — her boss — fired her.

After hearing the details of the case, Judge Simon Boussard of the Quebec Human Rights Tribunal fined the executive $7,000.

In response to the fine levied by the judge, the firm that employed the two fired the executive — and invited the female employee back to work, with no questions asked.

SEX, LIES, PANTIES, NEIGHBOURS AND VIDEOTAPE

OXFORD, MICHIGAN

SHE had a pretty good idea it was the dryer that was eating up her family's socks, but when it came to her panties, well, if she'd had any left they'd have certainly been tied in a knot.

Each week, another pair of her underwear went missing, and each week all this Oxford woman could do was shake her head.

Finally, when no other explanation seemed plausible, her husband set up a video camera on their premises which caught a neighbour sneaking into their house and nicking another pair of knickers.

Police called to the scene found over 100 pairs of panties and other articles of women's clothing in the neighbour's home.

"It blows your mind," the woman told a newspaper reporter. "We've lived next door for 15 years, and never had a clue. Out of 100 pairs of bloomers, 90 were mine."

If That's Lanolin I Smell on Your Breath, Ma'am, I'm Going to Have to Ask You to Come With Me

PORT-OF-SPAIN, TRINIDAD

IN a scene right out of *Doctor Dolittle*, police with guns drawn surrounded a car that they had been chasing through the countryside and discovered a small menagerie — a sheep and three goats, all nattily attired in dresses, shirts, pants, and fancy hats.

Police say they were investigating a farmer's complaint about missing livestock when they spotted a vehicle driving down a country lane with its lights out.

Officers say they were in pursuit of the car when the driver suddenly skidded to a stop and fled the scene on foot. Inside the vehicle, officers found a sheep wearing a blue and white dress, and a goat sporting a brightly colored shirt, trousers and a straw hat.

Two more goats clad in shirts and trousers were found cowering in the trunk.

Police suspect the rustler dressed the animals so the car's stolen occupants would look like a family, or a group of friends on their way to a party. Well, that's what they hoped.

Will the Two Men Beside the Water Cooler Please Step Forward

LIMA

THE expression *Good Cop, Bad Cop* has special meaning for Japanese businessman Masahito Ake.

While in Lima to take part in celebrations marking 100 years of Japanese immigration to Peru, Ake was grabbed from the street, forced at gunpoint into a car, and told by his captors to withdraw money from a midcity bank machine, "if he truly valued his life."

When his captors stopped to count their loot, the 40-year-old Japanese businessman got lucky.

He bolted from the kidnappers' car, hid until the two drove away, and eventually made his way to a police station where he got luckier still.

A sympathetic desk sergeant apologized, and explained to Masahito that corruption was everywhere. Even in the ranks of the police, he was about to add — and, as if to prove his point — who strolls into the police station but Masahito's kidnappers, now in their police uniforms, pockets bulging with ransom.

The two were arrested on the spot.

Beer Party!
I Thought You Said
Bear Party!

AMSTERDAM

WHEN police happened upon what looked like an adult bear sleeping on the shoulder of a highway, they naturally approached it with caution.

Closer inspection, including a gentle poking with a stick, revealed that the sleeper was in fact a young man in a bear suit.

He had been attending a nearby costume and beer drinking party and had decided to walk home.

The man said he had consumed about 15 pints of beer at the party when a boozy hibernation instinct came over him quite suddenly as he walked along the highway. He said he thought that if he lay down beside the road his friends would eventually see him and offer a lift.

Underneath the Lamp Post by the Barracks' Gate... Good Grief is That You Gerda?

BERLIN

POLICE were called into the red-light district here recently to break up an altercation that had broken out between Hans (not his real name) and Gerda (probably not her real name either).

Hans had been "wandering" (as some men will) through an area of the city frequented by prostitutes when he happened upon Gerda in the very early hours of the morning.

"What are you doing here?" asked Hans.

"What are you doing here?" asked Gerda.

The two, according to the officers who investigated the ensuing rhubarb, were husband and wife.

I Just Bought Two Tickets to Your Ball From Those Two Other Officers Down the Street

REYKJAVIK

ICELANDIC police were less than amused when they stopped a man for drunk driving and discovered they had stopped the same man an hour earlier for the same offence.

Following the original arrest at about 3 a.m., police shoved the besotted fellow into a taxi and told him to get on home.

Instead, one officer surmises, the drunk had the cabby take him to a friend's house where he borrowed a car, got behind the wheel and was driving erratically along another road when police pulled him over again.

No word yet on whether he made it safely home the second time. Or third.

Doctors Blame "Hi Mom" Syndrome for TV Confessions

ROCKFORD, ILLINOIS

MAYBE it was the booze talking, or the excitement of seeing a camera crew in his local tavern.

Or maybe it was that 15 minutes of prime time fame thing.

Whatever it was, a 22-year-old murder suspect ignored the Number One Rule of wanted fugitives — do not, we repeat, do not give live television interviews.

Police say Michael Zelmer couldn't resist the lure of the lights and the microphone in his face when asked for his views on the subject of underage drinking. Michael had opinions, plenty of them, and he not only shared them with the television audience, but also gave his real name when asked by the program's host.

Among the people watching the show was off-duty Police Detective Jim Barton who had seen this clown's mug and moniker on a police fax-bulletin just hours before.

Detective Barton dialed police headquarters, dispatching on-duty officers to Shooters Bar and Grill to make the arrest.

Okay, You Got All Six, But Even if I Give You Three Points for the Pedestrian — You Still Fail

TORONTO

SHE remembered to check both rearview and side mirrors before changing lanes.

She obeyed the speed limits and came to a complete stop at all intersections.

She was extra careful in the vicinity of crosswalks.

But the young lady crashed into six cars, and even pinned a pedestrian between two of them while attempting to park — all this during her driving test.

The teenager, according to police called to investigate the accident, rammed into four of the cars after she apparently hit the gas pedal instead of the brake, then rammed two more when she lost control of her vehicle for the second time.

The pedestrian was taken to hospital for treatment of leg injuries.

The driving inspector was treated for shock.

The teen failed to get her license.

You'll Find the Ugs-Dray in the Umpster-Day Behind the Ore-Stay Where They Sell the Ooze-Bay

HOLYOKE, MASSACHUSETTS

A man arrested on a charge of driving without a license used his one phone call to tell a friend exactly where he stowed a stash of crack cocaine.

Police say 30-year-old Hipolito Vega wanted his friend to bail him out with some quick drug money. So he spoke in Spanish, assuming no one else in the precinct would understand a word he said.

Turns out no one could — no one, that is, except Manuel Rivera, the booking officer, sitting across the desk from him.

With information from Officer Rivera, members of the drug squad got to the stash ahead of Vega's partner-in-crime and, sure enough, found six bags of crack cocaine exactly where Hipolito said they'd be.

Let's make that driving without a license, and possession of cocaine with intent to distribute.

IT WALKS LIKE A NUN, AND IT TALKS LIKE A NUN, BUT BE CAREFUL

BOGOTÁ, COLOMBIA

AUTHORITIES suspect that after seven break-ins in less than three months, the thief had convinced himself that the Sanctuary of the Virgin of Miracles was a pretty easy mark.

Wait for dark, climb the wall, help yourself to chickens from the sisters' flock, and maybe grab a religious relic or two to pawn if time allows.

What he never counted on, say police, was an armed and dangerous nun.

Local military commanders, worried about the safety of the small religious order stationed at the sanctuary, had provided the sisters with a revolver as well as a permit granting them permission to keep it on the premises.

The sisters, it turns out, must have added target practice to their daily routine.

While investigating strange noises in the corridors, one of the Sisters of the Sanctuary of the Virgin of Miracles opened fire, hitting the burglar right between the eyes, stopping him dead with one shot from her Smith & Wesson .38 special.

Oh brother!

Oh Sister!

File This One as:

Enticing, Confusing and Discombobulating the Enemy

LONDON

IN an all out effort to boost the morale of its armed forces, the British Ministry of Defence appears willing to go that extra inch or even, when necessary, to go where few men or women have had a chance to go before.

The Ministry of Defence recently announced it paid for a small number of female soldiers to have breast enlargements in order to make them happier. An army spokesperson said four women had received breast-enhancement surgery at one military hospital, and that this number was probably higher.

The Ministry of Defence also announced it will allow up to five members of the armed forces to undergo sex change operations carried out by the taxpayer-funded National Health Service.

She's not heavy, she's my brother … or something like that.

And We Did Not Even Need the Assistance of Inspector Clousseau

BORDEAUX, FRANCE

FRUSTRATED by a postal clerk whose cash box contained nothing close to the amount of money he was demanding, an armed and obviously frustrated bandit pulled out his bank card and asked to withdraw a lesser amount from his own account to make up for the difference.

Police say the would-be robber entered the post office waving his pistol in the air and demanded $13,000.

Told by the postal clerk that the bank did not have that kind of cash on hand, the bandit asked for $7,000.

When the clerk explained again that they did not have that much money, the man suggested he withdraw a lesser amount from his own account to compensate for the difference. He then handed over his bankcard to complete the illegal transaction.

Police officers who arrested him hours later had little trouble tracking him down. In all the confusion, the poor chap fled the bank, leaving his identity card behind.

PLEASE BE ADVISED THAT THE PETER PRINCIPLE STOPS HERE

BIRMINGHAM

A British clerical worker sued her employer and made headlines around the world when she was awarded more than $100,000 in compensation for being promoted.

Beverly Lancaster, a one-time Birmingham City office worker, said the promotion to a senior position triggered job-related stress that led to a need for early retirement.

Ruling in Ms. Lancaster's favour, Judge Frances Kirkham said she agreed that the promotion had led to mental illness.

At the hearing, Ms. Lancaster testified that she lacked the experience and qualifications to take on the new job, and that city council had failed to provide the training and support she felt was needed.

Don't Read This Item, We Repeat, DO NOT READ THIS ITEM

DES MOINES, IOWA

CALLING it an eyesore, officials hatched a plan aimed at cleaning up what one councillor called the "vulgar clutter" of lawn sale, garage sale and street sale signs affixed to utility poles throughout the city.

"Those things go up and they stay there long after the event they're promoting has come and gone," one committee member complained.

"I have telephone poles in my neighborhood that would fall down if you took the staples out of them," said another.

After much discussion about the high costs of promoting their plan in newspapers, on the radio and television, councillors opted instead to go the cheaper route — and posted NO SIGNS HERE notices on telephone and utility poles throughout the city.

Not Even When The Light Strikes Her in That Certain Way?

PHOENIX

O N the heels of seven armed robberies, including three in one afternoon, police issued an all points bulletin calling on officers throughout the city to be on the lookout for a "very ugly woman."

Police say the bandit's routine is always the same: pretending to be armed, the culprit demands cash, stuffs it into a ratty handbag, and flees on foot.

She is also described as having worn at least four different coloured wigs during her heists, and is said to sport very heavy makeup.

"She has been described by every victim as *a very ugly woman*," said a spokesperson for the Phoenix Police Department. "I know that sounds insulting, but maybe the description will tick her off and she'll call us."

Police, however, are keeping an open mind. "For all we know it could be an ugly man posing as an ugly woman."

HONK, IF YOU CAN READ WITHOUT MOVING YOUR LIPS

TORONTO

WHEN a Toronto motorist politely tooted his horn to tell the driver ahead of him that the light had changed, the driver quickly put down the newspaper he was reading and decided to teach that horn tooter a lesson or two.

First he flipped the other driver the ol' bird.

Next he fell in behind the horn tooter, and chased him a good distance along the highway.

Then he attempted to force him off the road.

It was about then the jerk discovered that the car he was attempting to force off the highway was an unmarked police cruiser, and the man behind the wheel was one of Toronto's finest.

According to the next day's edition of the very newspaper this clown was reading, his charges included both careless driving and dangerous operation of a motor vehicle.

I Think I'll Turn in, Love, Have You Seen My Bed Anywhere?

LONDON

A 62-year-old British husband walked out of a 38-year marriage and filed for divorce because he could no longer stand his wife's obsessive-compulsive behaviour — try as she did, she just couldn't stop moving their furniture around.

John Turner's application to end the marriage cited unreasonable behaviour.

He told the court that his wife, also 62, had been moving their chairs, tables, sofas, the television — anything not nailed down or fixed to the walls — every single day of their married lives, and that he just couldn't take it anymore.

The couple, the judge learned, even sold their house and bought a trailer, hoping it would break the wife's compulsive behaviour.

Pauline Turner does not contest the divorce, saying: "Moving furniture is just something I do. I imagine everybody has their little obsession."

The divorce was granted.

THAT'S MY STORY AND I'M STICKIN' TO IT

MADRID

PERHAPS he'd seen too many reruns of ol' Perry Mason who always seemed to save the day and his client's ass by producing that surprise witness with the airtight alibi.

Whatever it was, the young man charged with robbing a Madrid cab driver sat smiling and confident in the prisoner's dock as the prosecutor calmly unveiled an impressive mountain of evidence against him.

Asked at last if he had anything to say in his own defense, the fellow turned to the presiding magistrate, and with the confident air of a man with a rabbit up his sleeve, exclaimed that the prosecutor's case against him was laughable at best.

He most certainly could not have robbed the cab driver, the young man told the judge dramatically, for on the night in question he'd been picking pockets at a street fair in Seville, and furthermore, had witnesses who would swear to it.

TRUE OR FALSE
is Not The Answer,
It is the Question

SAN DIEGO

TWENTY-FIVE students at San Diego State University were given "F"s for cheating, and placed on probation after instructors discovered that they were cribbing the answers to a business quiz.

"What did I learn?" one of the students said to a newspaper reporter. "Obviously, not to cheat. It's not worth it."

Julie Logan, the university's judicial procedures officer said the number of students involved made the case an unusual one. "Most cheating brought to my attention involves a single student making the decision to cheat on his or her own."

The exam the cheating students faced?

Why, business ethics, of course.

That's Not Only the Biggest Dustball I've Ever Seen, it Seems to be Snoring

COWANSVILLE, QUEBEC

A 32-year-old burglar never dreamed he'd get caught — until police roused him from the deep sleep he was catching under a bed in the house he'd just broken into earlier that evening.

Police say the man triggered a silent alarm when he entered the home so had no idea that officers were on the way when he lay down to grab 40 winks.

Oddly, police missed him on their first search of the two-story bungalow.

"He had crawled under a bed we thought was too low for anyone to crawl under," said one officer, "so no one looked there."

It was a neighbour, helping the family clean up after police had left the premises, who called police back to the scene when she heard loud snoring in one of the bedrooms.

A police officer said the burglar was in such a deep sleep that they had difficulty waking him.

...And Atomic Bomb Beats Hand Grenade, and So it Goes Until Someone Gets Hurt

TORONTO

IN a clear case of the rock-scissors-paper game gone amok, a would-be hold-up artist was chased from a Toronto area discount store by a cashier who police say was singularly unimpressed by the wee kitchen knife brandished by the bandit.

The victim and his wife were both working in the downtown shop when the knife-wielding robber stormed through the front door demanding cash.

Investigators say that when the cashier asked if the man was serious, the suspect became agitated and began waving his little dagger in a threatening manner.

At this point, say police, the storekeeper reached under the counter, hefted a meat cleaver above his head and chased the lone bandit down the street.

Tune in Next Week for Another Installment of "There's a Light On, But..."

LETHBRIDGE, ALBERTA

WHEN it comes time to hand out the prize for their weekly *Not the Sharpest Knife in the Drawer* competition, police here admit the choice is seldom an easy one.

One week, for instance, they had this guy who pulled off the road just south of town and not only left his keys in his truck, but left the engine running while he dashed into the Roadhouse Bar.

But just when it looked like the truck owner might be the shoo-in of the week, police awarded the prize to the guy or guys who stole it and then abandoned it after a short joy ride — without even checking the glove compartment.

Inside the glove compartment — $3,000 in cash, left there by the owner!

I MUST WRITE NEATLY
I MUST WRITE NEATLY
I MUST WRITE NEATLY

PICKERING, ONTARIO

IF he walked into the station and wrote out a confession, say police in this bedroom community east of Toronto, it probably wouldn't stand up in court.

For starters, it's doubtful anyone could read it.

Police say that sloppy penmanship stymied a wanted fugitive's attempts to rob two local banks on two consecutive days.

In the first instance, the wannabe bandit simply ran from the bank empty-handed when the teller, try as she did, couldn't make out a single word of the hand-scrawled demand for cash.

The next day, at another bank down the street, a teller thought the note was asking if she had any large bills on hand. When she said no, again the frustrated fellow simply ran out the door.

Police are holding both hold-up notes as evidence, but say they are not even sure if a handwriting analyst could help.

UNSTABLE CONSTABLE TOLD TO TOE THE LINE

PORTLAND, OREGON

ONE year on the force and a Portland police officer was placed on medical leave and is "receiving treatment"— after two local women fingered him for attempting to forcibly suck their toes.

At his disciplinary hearing, it was pointed out that the constable's first victim — a sandal-clad espresso machine operator — yelled for help from a café window while the obviously obsessed young man hungrily smooched her toes and feet.

A short time later, a bartender at a nearby cocktail lounge reported a similar incident.

At the time of the alleged toe sucking, the randy rookie was off-duty and neither woman was aware that he was one of the city's finest.

A police representative says the young man had passed the standard background checks when he joined the force, but no history of similar behaviour had been recorded — not even a foot-note.

There Are No Openings Just Now, But If You'd Care to Leave a Resume…

SAN FRANCISCO

IS it possible that the man arrested for a series of heists turned to robbing banks when he couldn't find a job at one?

It's possible, say police, but highly unlikely.

More likely, however, is that the bank robber left his resume at the scene of the crime by accident, and not because he expected it to be kept on file.

"If you're going to drive a car, you shouldn't drink or do drugs, right?" said a police spokesperson. "Well, it's the same with robbing banks, and that's exactly what this guy was doing."

Described by four witnesses at four different banks as "drunk and disorderly," the 37-year-old bandit was arrested at his home when police found his name and address on a resume he had dropped during one of his capers.

Hey, I Don't Suppose We Have Time To Pick Up a Bag of Chocolate Chip Cookies, Eh?

KENTVILLE, NOVA SCOTIA

A 22-year-old pothead has added a cigarette lighter to the list of things he's hoping to get for his birthday, or for Christmas.

According to police, the out-of-province visitor was strolling along the Saturday night streets of this Annapolis Valley college town, when he stopped to ask a stranger for a light.

The stranger — a plainclothes police officer — obligingly flicked his Bic, caught a telltale whiff of that aromatic weed, and arrested the fellow on the spot.

Thieves Get the Chips, Cop Gets the Dip

HAMILTON, ONTARIO

WHEN a sharp-eyed police officer spotted a group of teenagers acting suspiciously in the vicinity of a trailer load of potato chips, he smelled trouble, and then some.

The thieves had indeed broken into the trailer, a police spokesman explained, and were making off with cartons of potato chips, when an officer interrupted them and immediately gave chase.

Unfortunately, the spokesman added, the thieves managed to get away when the fleet-footed flatfoot tripped in the dark and ended up — yep, right up to his armpits — in a septic tank filled with raw sewage.

All's well that ends well, however.

Police recovered the potato chips, and a civic-minded citizen gave the well-dipped policeman a lift home in the back of a pickup truck.

Driver, Take Me to the Scene of the Crime

NEW YORK

IF, as police would have us believe, some crooks are dumber than others, then we certainly owe a tip of the hat to this guy.

A dimwitted thief clambers into the back seat of a taxi, tells the driver where he wants to go, then several blocks later orders the driver out of the cab at knifepoint after robbing him of his day's earnings.

Police, acting on a hunch, check out the address that the thief had given the driver and sure enough, there he is.

"He might as well have asked the driver to take him to Rikers Island," said one of the arresting officers, referring to the infamous East River lockup.

This is Not What We Mean by Keeping An Eye On What's Behind, and An Eye On What's Ahead of Us Up The Road

BARRIE, ONTARIO

A young couple got a lecture on the rules of the road after police responded to several reports of a man driving naked along Highway 400, with a naked female passenger sitting in his lap, facing him.

While hurriedly donning their clothes, the couple told an astonished police officer that they assumed the tinted windows in their car were dark enough to prevent anyone from seeing in.

Not so, the officer explained, who later reported that driving naked, to the best of his knowledge, is not recommended in any drivers' manual he has ever seen, or by the Young Drivers of Canada association.

And Then, of Course, There are Those People Who Never Exhaled

STANWOOD, WASHINGTON

SOMETIMES police work is easy. Sometimes it's tough. And sometimes it's just plain weird. Writing out a ticket for indecent exposure, an officer asked a strange young man why he was wandering buck naked through the theatre district.

"I just feel like being naked, man," was the gist of the reply.

Something in that dreamy response prompted another officer to ask the fellow what he did for a living.

"I, like, grow marijuana, man," he told the officer and off they went where the now clothed wanderer walked police through a garden of 80 marijuana plants fastidiously concealed in a barn behind his home.

"It was … like … he was waiting for someone to tell his story to."

DON'T ANYBODY MOVE, THIS IS AN APOLOGY

FORT ST. JOHN, BRITISH COLUMBIA

AN armed bandit pulled off an early morning robbery at a convenience store, escaping with a moderate amount of cash and a really guilty conscience.

An employee told police she tackled the lone female bandit in an attempt to subdue her, but the wiry suspect broke free and ran from the store clutching a fistful of bills.

Police say officers at the scene of the crime were still interviewing the distraught clerk 20 minutes later when the rueful robber returned with the money and apologized for her behaviour.

Police, however, would offer no apologies for slapping her in cuffs.

Oh, He'll Climb Mountains, But When It's Time to Take Out The Garbage It's Like He's Got Two Broken Legs

LJUBLJANA, SLOVENIA

SLOVENIA'S top mountain climber returned home a hero after climbing one of the world's highest mountain peaks, then broke both his legs after falling into a hole in his backyard.

Tomaz Humar had accomplished what many had called the impossible — the first ever solo ascent of Dhaulagiri in the Nepalese Himalayas, the seventh highest mountain peak in the world.

The southern face of Dhaulagiri, which Humar climbed solo, is over 8,000 metres high.

The backyard excavation into which the 31-year-old mountain climber fell was three metres deep.

Parlez-Vous "This is a Stick Up"

OTTAWA

WHAT with French immersion, English immersion, and language legislation sponsored by federal and provincial governments, bilingualism is a fact of life in most parts of Canada.

So when a 27-year-old would-be bank robber crossed the river into the province of Quebec to ply his trade, he naturally expected to do business in the language of his choice.

Ah well, as they say in French, *plus ça change.*

The culprit handed his hold-up note to a young teller who couldn't read a single word of English, so off she went to ask a co-worker for a translation.

Apparently sensing that things were going from *tres* bad to *tres* worse, the red-faced bandit suddenly bolted out the front door of the bank and into the back seat of a waiting taxi.

With a description from bank staff, and the cabbie, police arrested the suspect in downtown Ottawa only hours later.

Teens Swoop and Scoop, But Dog Owner Gets Last Laugh

DES MOINES, IOWA

THREE smart-ass teenagers shouted "thank you" as they grabbed an enticing-looking package that a lady had placed on the trunk of her car as she struggled with her keys.

"Your welcome," she shouted back as the laughing trio made its getaway.

"I wish I could be there when they open it up," the lady told a police constable who chanced by.

Prior to the incident, the woman had been walking her terrier in a nearby park, and the package stolen from her contained a long walk's worth of stooping and scooping — a tidy packet of soggy doggy-do.

I Knew Elmer The Safety Elephant, And You, Sir, Are No Elmer!

TORONTO

POLICE have long been used to delivering messages on safety, lawfulness, and good citizenship to schoolchildren.

From "talking" police cars that preach good driving habits, to tours of jails to impress upon young minds the consequences of breaking the law — the contributions of our men and women in blue have played an important role in spreading the gospel of proper behaviour.

It is not surprising then that parents and teachers alike were aghast to learn that an Ontario Provincial Police Officer in charge of chaperoning pre-teens had been suspended for going where others, we'd like to think, have never gone before.

Perhaps he felt that looking both ways before crossing the street was too old hat for this particular audience. Maybe he was afraid they would consider his lecture on seatbelt safety a waste of time.

Whatever the reasons, police officials say the officer was suspended for one day without pay for showing his young charges how to make "blue angels" by dropping his trousers and passing gas over the flame of a cigarette lighter held dangerously close to his keister.

I Think We Got Another Cousin On Your Mother's Side Who Just Might Be Willing

PLYMOUTH, WISCONSIN

TWO bored teenagers who had always wondered what it might feel like to get shot, now know, thanks to a somewhat dim relative who agreed to do the shooting for them.

You read it right.

It was just one of those hot, boring summer days, according to Captain David Adams of the Sheboygan County Sheriff's Office, when the boys — 17-year-old cousins — got to talking about getting shot and what it might feel like.

As best as Capt. Adams can reconstruct, it was then that one of the youngsters remembered a none-too-swift 34-year-old relative down the road who just might oblige.

And sure enough, he did.

The 34-year-old was arrested when the boys showed up for medical treatment at two different area hospitals.

None of the three was identified, pending the outcome of charges.

Robber Leaves Loonies, Toonies, and Other Assorted "Clue-Nies" For Police

NORTHBRIDGE, MASSACHUSETTS

POLICE say the eyes and ears of an observant employee helped them run down the perpetrator of an armed robbery at a local doughnut shop, but then admitted to reporters that one of the bandits was no genius when it came to concealing the clues officers needed to solve the crime.

The masked robber, a former employee, did nothing to disguise his distinctive voice, which was recognized immediately by a staffer who had worked with him at the all-night eatery.

Also, his accomplice, the victim explained, carelessly called the crook by his nickname — "A.J." — throughout the heist.

And finally, from the sports bag in which he toted his loot, A.J. left a trail of coins that police were able to follow from the doughnut shop straight to his apartment building two doors away.

Police recovered $1,400 in cash, two ski masks, a hatchet and a tire iron, and offered A.J. a half-dozen honey-glazed for the name and address of his partner-in-crime. A.J.'s chewing the offer over.

This Is Not at All Humorous, You Will Stop Laughing Immediately

BERLIN

A German magazine reports that approximately half the men taking part in a recent study complain that standard European Union sized condoms are too big for German men.

The study, published in *Focus* magazine, suggests that 50% of readers say the standard-sized condoms keep falling off.

"The average German penis appears to be approximately 3.5 to 4 millimeters too narrow for the standard condoms," the magazine reports.

The European Union set the standard for condoms in 1996 to establish uniform sizes for prophylactics — and thousands of other products — throughout Europe.

Several unsigned letters to the editor demand to know which country supplied the "standard-sized" penises used as models in the manufacturing process.

Comment Dit Vous En Francais, "Dumb Bunny?"

MONTPELLIER, FRANCE

A 44-year-old Frenchman drove to a local lockup to console his younger brother who had just been arrested for drunk driving — and ended up sharing his brother's cell, charged with the same offense.

Police say the first driver failed his breathalyzer test at a roadside check and was booked immediately.

Jailers, concerned about the erratic behaviour of the visiting brother, ordered him to take a breathalyzer which he too failed with flying colours.

Frère et frère spent the night in jail.

WE TOLD HIM A HUNDRED TIMES — TIMING, STEVIE, TIMING IS EVERYTHING!

SPARTANBURG, SOUTH CAROLINA

BEING in the right place at the right time is something upon which we can all agree.

Being in the wrong place at the wrong time is another matter all together.

A 24-year-old robber can vouch for that.

The young man had just knocked over a corner store, and while making his getaway flagged down a passing car for a quick lift from the scene.

"Take me to the Krispy Kreme doughnut shop," the bandit demanded.

But, no. The vehicle turned out to be an unmarked police car.

The driver turned out to be a plainclothes police officer.

And the would-be robber turned up in court the next day, charged with armed robbery.

When Last Seen The Suspect Was Wearing a Silly Grin

TORONTO

IT took police just over a month to catch up to a 20-year-old car thief after he escaped custody by bolting from a police-station shower. When the cops finally did apprehend the little rascal, he was still as buck naked as the day he was born — and the day he escaped.

Police say that as they struggled to arrest the panicky young man the first time, he defecated in his trousers, and was then taken to the shower room at police headquarters.

Instead of using the opportunity to take a shower, the thief took a powder through an unlocked security door and ran off down the street.

Acting on a tip a full month later, the police were more than a little amused to find the fellow still *au naturel*, this time at a downtown tanning parlour.

Arresting New Novel Might be the Next Smash Hit

BROCKVILLE, ONTARIO

WHEN an Ontario Provincial Police Officer spotted a young lady driving erratically along a busy stretch of four-lane highway, he decided to check it out.

Pulling his flashing vehicle into the lane behind her, the officer noted that the lady driver never as much as glanced in her rearview mirror, and continued to drive as though she was the only person on the road.

Positioning his cruiser alongside her sedan and paralleling it for what seemed like several minutes, the patrolman noted there was still no reaction from the driver despite his frantic signals for her to pull over.

It was then that he noticed she was reading a book.

On comes the siren, the lady pulls onto the shoulder of the road, and the officer charges her with careless driving.

When asked by a reporter, a police spokesperson said the officer did not include the title of the book in his report.

Forget Park Avenue, Forget Boardwalk, and Go Directly Back To Jail

FORDYCE, ARKANSAS

SOMETIMES even the best ideas aren't worth the brain they're etched on.

Take Sherman Lee Parks.

If Sherman had known what was happening in the judge's chambers that day, he'd have been a free man.

But Sherman didn't know what was going on, so the idea of busting out of jail seemed like a good one, maybe even the best one he'd had all day.

What he didn't know, of course, was that at the very moment he was busting out of jail, a Jefferson County judge was signing his release papers.

The judge had decided the nine months Sherman served for burglary was time enough, it seems.

Sherman was back in jail the very next day, charged with escaping custody and being at large.

Elvis Is In The Building, But He's Gone To Bed

FORT MCMURRAY, ALBERTA

THEY'RE calling it "Jailhouse Rock — The Sequel."

In what appears to have been a blatant attempt to be included in this book, a 23-year-old man told a judge that he sometimes drinks too much and does stupid things.

The judge accepted the young man's guilty plea and levied a fine of $345 for what court officials agree was a pretty dumb stunt.

Police say the young man and a friend were arrested shortly after midnight when they were found banging on a window and attempting to break — not out of — but into a nearby prison.

The Crown prosecutor told the court that, when confronted, the two said they were there "to party with Randy."

Jailers say that to the best of their knowledge, Randy slept through the entire incident.

Purpose of Loan? Hmm, How 'bout Getaway Car and the Cost of Relocating

NEW ROCHELLE, NEW YORK

PRETENDING she was there on legitimate business, and while summoning up the nerve for the job, a 39-year-old would-be bank robber sat down in an office and filled out an application for a loan.

Then she robbed the place, and out the door she fled with $10,000.

According to police officers who arrested her less than an hour later, she should probably have applied for some brains instead of dough.

Turns out, Lucille Amaore, who lives less than two blocks away from the bank, filled out the loan application using her own name and address.

MAN WANTS SEX CHANGE OPERATION REVERSED...
Just Like a Woman

TEHRAN

IT'S not because a woman's work is never done; it has nothing to do with getting paid less than a man for work of equal value.

And it's not that Maryam is sick and tired of being a sex object.

Known as Mehran prior to his sex change operation, the 25-year-old Iranian says he wants the operation reversed because life as a woman in Iran is simply unbearable.

The former gentleman says that after 24 years as a man, he regretted becoming a woman almost immediately, finding it simply too difficult to live with the dress and social restrictions placed on women in the conservative Islamic nation.

"Let's just say I've changed my mind," he said, she said.

My Name is Bill and I Am an Armed Bandit

FORT SMITH, ARKANSAS

CRIME fighters the world over say there are two things to remember when confronted by criminals, or when witnessing a crime.

Don't be a hero.

And do try to remember everything you can about the perpetrators.

Mary Buckner can vouch for that.

Police responding to the holdup of a local convenience store say Mary, the lady behind the counter, was a big help in solving this particular armed robbery.

She was able to describe the pistol pointed at her, the hard hat worn by the gentleman in question, the colour of his getaway car, and she even remembered his name — which was neatly stenciled above the bill of his hard hat.

Case closed.

Do You, Mustang Sally, Take This Here Good Ol' Boy, Buster Mitchell...

KNOXVILLE, TENNESSEE

JILTED by his girlfriend, this southern boy's contingency plan to marry the other big love in his life was spoiled when a courthouse clerk explained that only men and women can get properly hitched under Tennessee law.

Describing himself as "broken hearted," Buster Mitchell had arrived at the clerk's office hell-bent on getting hitched to his 1996 Mustang GT.

"In California they are doing same-sex marriages," Mitchell complained. "So why can't we do the *good ol'* boy thing right here in Tennessee and marry our cars or our trucks?"

The courthouse clerk who rained on the 28-year-old bachelor's parade says he became suspicious when reading the application for the wedding license. Buster had recorded his fiancé's birthplace as "Detroit," her father as "Henry Ford" and her blood type as "10-W-40."

What's That Expression... "They're Never Around When You Need Them" – Except at the Doughnut Shop

WINNIPEG

OBVIOUSLY unaware of the cultural link between cops and crullers, three Bosnian refugees were arrested right here in Canada while — you got it — attempting to rob a doughnut shop.

The three masked men had emptied the cash register at Robin's Doughnuts and were about to flee the premises when two on-duty constables "just got that craving."

"We just happened to be in the right place at the right time," said one of the policemen.

Caught off guard, and obviously more than a little surprised by the arrival of the two constables, the confused delegation surrendered without incident.

If English as a Second Language (ESL) is offered in the clink, these three wannabe bandits might also want to consider brushing up on the customs, cuisine, and eating habits of their Canadian hosts.

Better Call in a Backup, Charlie, I Don't Like the Smell of This

EDMONTON

S USPECTING a robbery in progress, six police cruisers forced an armored van to a halt after witnesses reported a guard signaling frantically for help as the vehicle sped erratically along a city street.

Witnesses say the guard was repeatedly swinging the vehicle's door open and shut in what appeared to be an attempt to attract attention.

A police spokesman later cleared the air when he explained to reporters that one of the guards had just passed gas and the other guard was simply attempting to ventilate the cab by flapping its door open and closed.

We Should Very Much Like to Apologize for Making Your Trip a Pleasant One

LONDON

A British train passenger was startled and confused when two letters of apology arrived on his doorstep just days after he wrote the railway company to express his appreciation for its exemplary service.

In an addition to an apology, the first letter from Richard Branson's Virgin Trains also offered a refund.

The second letter apologized further for not dealing with the rider's complaint in a timely manner.

Railway officials blame a temporary employee for the mixup, and say the form-letter apologies should not be interpreted as an automatic, or "trained" response.

THAT'S JAMES, JESSE JAMES

OSWEGO, NEW YORK

WHAT'S in a name? Not much, it seems. He's Jesse James all right, but any other links between this 18-year-old robbery suspect and the legendary 1880s bank robber seem to have dissolved in the family gene pool.

Police say the thoroughly modern Jesse James used his shopper's bonus card to get a discount on goods purchased at a local grocery store, and when that transaction was complete, pulled a pellet gun from under his jacket and demanded cash.

James and two accomplices fled the store with $600, but the hapless 18-year-old was traced, tracked down and arrested as soon as police retrieved his name and address from the store's bonus card scanner.

That Depends on What Your Definition of Crime (Or Egg) Is

ONTARIO, CALIFORNIA

A candidate for the U.S. Congress was held up at gunpoint minutes after he declared on television that crime was only the figment of his opponent's imagination, and neither a problem nor an issue in his suburban district.

Independent candidate Hale McGee and his campaign manager had just finished tacking a campaign poster above a payphone at a gas bar when two men — one armed with a handgun — accosted them and demanded money.

The two crooks then drove off, leaving candidate McGee to reconsider the issues.

Said McGee, "I feel like I have egg all over me."

This is the Weather Network, and You are Getting *HOT, HOT, HOT*

TORONTO

A Grade 4 teacher thought he had called 1-800-0MY-GOSH after dialing the number printed in his students' introductory algebra text.

"Nobody checked this book out," said the embarrassed instructor when the number in the textbook turned out, not to be the Weather Network's feedback service, but an extremely wordy gay male chat line.

The teacher says he dialed the number listed in the book and, to keep the students interested and involved, began to repeat out loud the words he was hearing from the other end of the line.

Suddenly realizing what was happening, the teacher decided that the sweet nothings being whispered into his ear were not terribly suitable for his students and hung up.

KNOCK KNOCK
There's No Joke in This Jewelry Store Robbery

TORONTO

POLICE say an inattentive accomplice in the robbery of a downtown jewelry store could probably have laid claim to a reward if he had ignored his partner's frantic signals just a little bit longer.

The plan, it seems, was that one of the robbers would enter the store on the pretence of buying a diamond ring, then signal his partner to come in for the heist. The signal, the jewel thief apparently decided, would be to bang himself on the back of the head, thus indicating that the jeweler had laid out an assortment of rings on the counter top.

Suddenly, he began to signal his partner, but according to police, his partner was looking elsewhere.

Whack, whack. Bang, bang. And the frantic signaling continued. Yet still no response from his accomplice.

"The guy keeps whacking himself on the back of his head," a witness told reporters. "He must have given himself a migraine."

Finally, the second robber spotted the signal and came racing into the shop. Another few minutes, a reporter mused, and the fellow might have knocked himself out.

The pair fled the store with rings valued at several hundred thousand dollars — a haul most crooks would consider well worth the headache.

Different Definitions of Light Reading

WINNIPEG

WHEN it comes to literary taste, say the people who run our jails and penitentiaries, Canadian convicts are every bit as eclectic as the rest of us.

Check any cell, and the selection of reading matter you find will range from bibles to bestsellers, from potboilers to paperback porn.

Not surprising then that when jailers confiscate his *Funk & Wagnall's Canadian College Dictionary*, inmate James Skinner gets into a shouting match.

"I can have as many dirty books as I want, but I can't have a dictionary!" he protests through his lawyer.

In the war of words, however, the warden has the final say.

Jail officials refuse to budge, saying a tome that large and that heavy could easily be used as a weapon.

Ah, the power of words.

WANTED: A FEW BAD MEN

BOSTON

LURED with the promise of easy money, more than 100 con men and various bunco artists were tricked into attending a fake "job fair" where they were promptly arrested by police on outstanding warrants for crimes that included assault, robbery, drug offenses, welfare fraud and child support violations.

The sting operation — three months in the planning — began with letters from a phony employment agency offering high paying jobs and union benefits to workers selected for the city's massive "Big Dig" construction project.

Those who answered the letters were invited to the "job fair," told to be on time and told to be sure to bring along some form of photo ID.

Police aren't certain if it was the opportunity to work on the historic project, or maybe just the novelty of a day's pay for an honest day's toil, but say many of the fugitives arrived in high spirits, and seemed genuinely anxious to get to work.

Some even brought along friends who also were being sought by police, a spokesperson said.

Suffice to say, all were arrested on the spot.

With No One To Carp To, Protesters Clam Up and Go Home

ATLANTIC CITY

THEY waved banners reading "Don't Batter Me" and shouted at each other about the need to create a better world for the creatures of the sea.

"Gill" the fish was there — a six-foot tall man in a fish suit.

And so too were members of People for the Ethical Treatment of Animals.

They had gathered at Dock's Oyster House, a 102-year-old landmark restaurant, to kick off their anti-seafood campaign, and raise awareness about live lobsters being plunged into boiling water, and oysters being eaten alive.

The only thing missing was an audience.

Dock's, the city's oldest seafood restaurant, is closed at lunchtime, so there were no customers to lobby.

"How were we to know they don't serve lunch," said one of the organizers as the protesters packed up and headed home. "We don't eat seafood."

ARE YOU JUST HAPPY TO SEE ME, OR IS THAT WHAT I THINK IT IS?

PARIS

CUSTOMS officials first became suspicious of a passenger disembarking a flight from Colombia when the man began squirming and twitching nervously while being questioned.

They became doubly suspicious, a spokesperson says, when an airport security sniffer dog became skittish and wouldn't approach within several metres of the man despite his handler's commands.

Under further questioning by airport police, the fellow produced a 40-centimetre long baby boa constrictor, which he had been trying to smuggle into the country in his underwear.

Police confiscated the snake, explaining that the importation of exotic pets is against the law in France. Men's thong bathing suits, however, are still permitted on France's public beaches.

Empty Headed Crooks Forget Fill Up During Stick Up

EAST PEORIA, ILLINOIS

TWO wannabe hold-up artists were arrested minutes after their getaway car ran out of gas and sputtered to a stop less than two blocks from the scene of their crime — a downtown gas bar.

Police say that instead of hailing a cab, or fleeing on foot, the two men walked a kilometre to another service station where they purchased a can of gas and then — loaded down with the gas and the loot from the robbery — walked straight back to the getaway car where they were arrested and charged.

Said one of the arresting officers, "Why they didn't get a fill up while robbing the gas station is anybody's guess."

BABY, LET ME LIGHT A FIRE

PETERBOROUGH, ONTARIO

FIRST she sets his heart on fire.

Then the relationship goes up in smoke.

Then his house burns to the ground.

No, it's not Hank Williams Junior, or Billy Ray Cyrus, or even Johnny Cash.

And NO — not just another "Dear John" hurting and fuming about another "old flame" who's done him wrong.

This angry young man was treated for burns at an area hospital after a paint can exploded while he was burning his ex-girlfriend's belongings in his fireplace.

Police believe it was while the man was being treated at hospital that the fire spread, destroying the house and everything in it.

And For The Lovely Bride, Two Minutes For Roughing

MONTREAL

FIRST it was cupid's arrow, then the left hook, and the young man, as they sometimes say in the arena of love, didn't know what hit him.

But down he went.

And a boozing, brawling 27-year-old Montreal bride pleads guilty in a Montreal courtroom to punching out her husband on their wedding day.

Police, called to break-up a fight at a wedding, assumed that one or more of the wedding guests had over imbibed during the reception and got rowdy.

Instead, said police, they ended up witnessing the aftermath of a fight between bride and groom.

The blushing bride was fined $300 for assault and public mischief. The groom filed for divorce four days later.

C'est la vie. C'est la guerre.

I Love the Smell of Burning Money in the Morning

MONTREAL

FOUR would-be robbers watched their dreams go up in smoke when a nightmare of bad luck and bad timing interrupted their daring daytime robbery of an armoured truck.

Things got off to a bad start when heat from a blowtorch the crooks were using to slice through the doors of the armoured vehicle set fire to the money inside.

Next thing they knew, flames from the burning money spread, setting the entire truck on fire.

This larger fire then triggered the van's alarm system.

And finally, as the hapless quartet was speeding away from their scene of woe, a police SWAT team swooped down out of nowhere and arrested them without a struggle.

Adding insult to injury, a police spokesman told the press that the four bandits — suspects in the robberies of at least two other armoured vehicles — were under police surveillance every step of the way.

Said one officer at the press briefing, "I've heard of money burning a hole in somebody's pocket, but this was something else."

Well, Since You're Going There Anyway, Would You Mind Delivering These

ORILLIA, ONTARIO

POLICE charged an Orillia teenager with speeding and several other driving offences when a roadside radar unit clocked him at 194 kilometres an hour — a speed that is more than 100 km/h over the 90 km/h limit.

When questioned at the scene, the 18-year-old Mario Andretti wannabe admitted that no, he was not a volunteer fireman racing to a fire, or a panicky husband attempting to get his pregnant wife to the hospital before her next contraction.

Turns out the young man was running late for — and we kid you not — an appointment with a company that specializes in fighting speeding tickets.

Stay tuned.

"That's 15 Doughnuts" Nudge Nudge, Wink Wink, Know What I Mean

HALIFAX

TWO 19-year-olds were busted for selling marijuana at a local drive-through doughnut shop when the secret password they coined for their special customers just didn't cut it in the world of cinnamon and crullers.

With doughnuts, people generally order in even numbers — a half dozen or a dozen at a time, explained a Tim Horton's spokesperson about the etiquette of doughnut exchange.

"Suddenly, cars are pulling up to the speaker and ordering "15" Timbits. Like c'mon, naturally our manager gets suspicious."

Suspicious enough to intercept one of those orders, police say, and to call them immediately when she discovered a coffee cup of cannabis.

The order for "15" doughnuts obviously meant that the customer was looking to *roll up more than the rim*, and start the day on something stronger than a sugar high.

You Say Your Head Hurts on the Left Side... Now Would That be My Left, or Yours?

WASHINGTON

A South Carolina doctor who used a patient's amputated foot in a crab trap, and a Florida surgeon who began a brain operation by cutting into the wrong side of his patient's head, are among the more than 20,000 doctors listed as "questionable" by the consumers' group, Public Citizen.

In the 2000 edition of its annual report, Public Citizen names 20,125 doctors and some 28,000 disciplinary actions taken against them for offences ranging from having sex with patients to income tax evasion.

The South Carolina doctor and part-time crab fisherman was fined $3,000 and reprimanded. The Florida surgeon was fined $6,000 and ordered to take five hours of additional medical education.

Both doctors are still practicing.

Read Me That Part About the Birds and the Bees Again

DELRAY BEACH, FLORIDA

WITH 6 children, 14 grandchildren, and 17 great-grandchildren between them, 90-year-old Max Gordon and his 82-year-old fiancée Molly Levy would seem unlikely to need a book on parenting, but in Florida, the law's the law.

And the law in question is the state's *Marriage Preparation and Preservation Act of 1998*, put on the books to protect children in the event of, and from the effects of, failed marriages.

When the couple went to pick up their marriage license, according to Molly, a young clerk handed them the book.

"I said what's it about, and she said 'parenting,' and so we read it because we thought there might be a test," said Molly, adding that she had to read the book to Max because of his failing eyesight.

Pit Bulls, You Say? Aren't They the Ones Born Without a Sense of Humour?

AMSTERDAM

"RUFF, RUFF," the 43-year-old drunk barked at the dog to the amusement of onlookers in the market square. "Please don't do that," said the dog's owner.

"Ruff, ruff, ruff," the drunk continued, laughing and getting down on all fours, the better to confront and tease the dog.

"Please, stop," the dog's owner begged, but to no avail.

It was when the man attempted to rub noses with the nervous pup, witnesses told police, that the dog reacted instinctively, lunging at his pesky attacker and biting a chunk out of his nose.

"I don't know what kind of dog he thought it was," said a medic called to the scene, "but he obviously had no idea that it was a pit bull terrier."

Hell, When I Was Yer Age We Used to Steal Cars in Six Feet of Snow… Uphill…in Reverse

TORONTO

POLICE say a 16-year-old would-be car-jacker was stymied in his attempt to steal a car in a downtown parking lot when, after shoving the car's owner aside and leaping into the driver's seat, he discovered that the vehicle had a standard shift.

Brandishing a knife, the frustrated young man attempted to force a passer-by to drive the car for him, police say, then fled the scene when his threats were ignored.

The youth was arrested attempting another theft a short time later.

Commenting on a perceived increase in teenage criminality, a local radio announcer referred to the 16-year-old's car-jacking attempt as an obvious case of "gear pressure."

When Gene Pools and Car Pools Go Bad

CAMBRIDGE, ONTARIO

THE husband and wife who drink together could end up in the clink together, say Cambridge police after a bizarre roadside spot check results in two charges of impaired driving — involving the same car!

Officers say they stopped the car, which had been weaving erratically along the highway, and asked the driver to accompany them to the cruiser for routine questioning.

It was while they were questioning the driver that the husband — who had been waiting in the passenger seat of the stopped vehicle — suddenly jumped behind the wheel and took off down the highway.

Police gave chase, stopped the car, and arrested the husband.

The pair are charged with impaired driving — the husband with additional counts of resisting arrest and driving without a license.

The arresting officers finished their shift, and went home to bed convinced that the world will never be totally free of looniness.

SORRY, SIR, BUT YOUR CONNECTION HAS BEEN PERMANENTLY DISFIGURED

GRAFTON, OHIO

A 29-year-old woman, tired of her husband's constant on-line chatting, was fined $200 for "hacking" into his computer terminal — with a meat cleaver.

Kelli Michetti was fined $200 after pleading "no contest" to a charge of domestic violence and resisting arrest.

The young woman told police that her husband seemed more interested in talking to women in "chat rooms" than he was in talking to her, often not even coming to bed until 4 a.m.

She said she had at first attempted to chop off the power line on the machine, but instead attacked the terminal itself during the escalating argument with her husband.

Round The Bend
She Drove Me, Crazy,
and Then Into Debt

BEDFORD, PENNSYLVANIA

A 44-year-old Bedford man accepted a ride to court with his estranged wife only to be arrested and charged with contempt for violating a judge's order forbidding him from having any contact with her.

The man explained that he only accepted the lift because he was running late for his meeting with the judge.

A court official said the husband and wife were on their way to see the judge to discuss the previously imposed restraining order.

Releasing the man on $1,000 bail, Judge Thomas Ling explained that a "restraining order is a restraining order" and must be obeyed no matter what the circumstance.

The hearing to discuss the restraining order was rescheduled. The husband says he'll get there on his own this time.

Stick That Under the Seat in Front of You, or in the Overhead Rack

MIRAMICHI, NEW BRUNSWICK

TALK about a bundle of love.

Armed with just a bit more ardour than ready cash, two young lovers were more than a little embarrassed when their plans for a romantic weekend getaway went awry.

The coach was loading for Moncton, a transportation company official said, when baggage handlers discovered a wiggling duffel bag among the totes and suitcases they were tossing into the luggage hold beneath the bus.

Unzipping the bag, they found a blushing 22-year-old man attempting to get a free ride while his girlfriend travelled in style.

Witnesses mused that the couple undoubtedly decided against flying for fear the airlines might lose the young lady's baggage.

WARNING:
The Surgeon General Has Determined That Smoking Can Blow Your Head Off

BANGKOK

NO one was seriously hurt, but more than thirty celebrities, dignitaries, and anti-smoking activists were left with singed hair and eyebrows when a huge mock cigarette exploded during an anti-smoking ceremony at a Bangkok shopping mall.

Hundreds of shoppers cheered popular singer Payong Mukda as he attacked the 10-metre long cigarette with a sword to kick off World No-Smoking Day.

They cheered even louder when the entertainer, unable to slice the evil weed in half, resorted to stabbing it through and through.

And then, they recoiled in horror as the giant cigarette suddenly caught fire and exploded on the stage.

Police suspect a spark from the sword striking the metal stage ignited hundreds of gas-filled balloons, which were used to stuff the monster cigarette.

That's Mick, and That's Keef and Ron, But Who's That Short Bald Guy?

ORLANDO, FLORIDA

CLOSE, but that's no cigar.
A Florida woman, showing off photos she had taken at last night's rock concert, was shocked to discover pictures of a man's penis among her souvenir snaps.

So was her sister, and a friend who promptly marched the offending portraits off to the local police station where she filed a formal complaint.

The ladies told police that they were unable to get within 50-metres of the stage, so they turned their camera over to an obliging Orlando police officer who offered to make his way through the crowd and get "close-ups" of the band.

Instead, it turned out, the constable had taken several photos of his partner's privates before returning the camera to the thankful fans.

When confronted by superiors, both officers confessed to the tasteless prank, and were disciplined.

You Will Stand in Line and Show Some Identification or You Will Not Be Served

BERLIN

A 31-year-old hold-up artist ran headfirst into red tape when a bank teller refused to hand over the loot without ID.

Like many offices throughout Germany, Deutsche banks demand ID cards for even the most routine business transactions, so police say it is not surprising that when a young teller asked the pistol-packing bandit for his, he obeyed.

What is surprising, they say, is that after scooping up a small amount of cash, the fellow fled the bank, leaving his identification behind.

The man was arrested a few hours later, charged with robbery and extortion.

Bureaucracy 1. Bank Robber 0.

The modest teller received top marks for coolness under pressure from her employers and the police, but shrugged off the praises of her fellow employees saying she was just following orders.

Hi, My Name is Constable Logan and I'll Be Your Arresting Officer Tonight

EDMONTON

AFTER failing in their attempt to hold-up a diner at knifepoint, two hungry bandits accepted the chef's offer of a meal on the house, and were sitting at the counter, patiently waiting for their food when police arrived and took them into custody.

The chef told police that the pair had entered the restaurant on the pretext of ordering sandwiches, then pulled a knife on him and demanded cash.

Instead of obeying their demands, said the cook, he triggered the lock on the cash register and set off the alarm.

When the duo dashed from the premises, the chef gave chase while shouting out his offer of free sandwiches.

"Most people's gut instinct would be to flee the scene," mused one police officer. "But I guess the gut instinct in this case was hunger."

From The Oven to the Frying Pan to the Fire and Back

SAN JOSE, CALIFORNIA

IT was the perfect getaway.

Police say inmate Arnold Ancheta escaped from the Elmwood Correctional Facility by carving footholds in the wall above his bunk.

Then, as nearly as they can reconstruct it, Arnold climbed the wall and used a broom handle to pry apart the bars over the skylight in the ceiling of his cell.

Next, it appears, he squeezed through the bars, removed the Plexiglas skylight, and climbed onto the roof of the medium security wing in which he was being held.

Free at last, the 25-year-old jumped six metres below in one final leap toward freedom. Unfortunately, he vaulted the wrong fence and ended up in the women's jail next door.

Spotting poor Arnold limping about their playground, female inmates alerted correctional officers who hurried him off to hospital for ankle injuries, then back to jail.

Alright Mister, You've Stolen Your Last Sock

CHIPPEWA FALLS, WISCONSIN

A 37-year-old man was arrested for endangering public safety after police say he pushed his washing machine down the stairs during a temper tantrum, and then filled it full of holes.

The man was charged with discharging a weapon within 30 metres of a residential dwelling after neighbours reported hearing shots.

Police say the washing machine bounced down the stairwell from the man's second floor apartment and rolled into the driveway. The man then drew his .25 calibre pistol, moseyed on up to the dastardly appliance and proceeded to fill the sock-eating varmint full of lead.

Guy Boos told officers he was angry with the appliance. No one knows if he had consulted the Maytag Repair Man before the incident.

How Many Robbers Could Four Robbers Rob If Four Robbers...

SAO PAULO, BRAZIL

IF they ever catch up with them, you can be rest assured that the prisoners in Tremembe Jail will have a few choice words for the mean-spirited bandits who broke into their prison and ran off with their hard-earned cash.

According to prison officials, four armed men got into the prison by overpowering the guards, then entered an administrator's office and made off with cash that the inmates had been socking away from jobs inside and outside the prison.

"Bandits robbing convicts is appalling," commented one prison guard, explaining that the convicts had been saving the money — approximately 50,000 reais ($28,000 US) — to mail home for Father's Day.

A police officer in Tremembe was more philosophical. "Money is money," he mused. "There are not too many places to rob around here." Tremembe, where the prison is located, is a town of approximately 30,000 people about 150 kilometres north of Sao Paulo.

Crouching Tiger, Hidden, Screaming, Kicking, Dangerous Karate Champion

COLOMBO, SRI LANKA

WHAT do you call it when four hopped-up louts drag two women into the woods and the two women emerge only minutes later — laughing?

Well, if you are one of the four Sri Lankan men involved — and you can still manage it — you might consider calling for help.

Or, according to the Colombo *Daily News*, you just might call it poetic justice.

Police say the young women were walking along the highway near the town of Matale when four thugs confronted them, and then hauled them into the bushes alongside the road.

It was there and then, police say, that the assailants discovered that one of the young ladies was the newly crowned Grand Winner of the Open Karate Championships just held in India.

The four men fled the assault scene on foot but were arrested nearby — two of them, according to police — still limping badly.

Polly Wants a Lawyer
Polly Wants a Phone Call
Polly Knows Her Rights

MONTREAL

MONTREAL police admit they'd normally bring a search warrant for a bust like this, but instead entered an apartment without one when a "little birdie" told them to come on in.

Called to an apartment building to investigate a report of two dogs running about the premises without leashes, officers were directed to the door of an apartment where other tenants said the owner of the dogs resided.

Officers knocked on the door.

A voice said, "Come in."

And in they went.

Inside the apartment, police discovered they were talking to a parrot. They also discovered a "garden" of more than 40 marijuana plants.

Officers say they chatted with the parrot until the tenant showed up, and then arrested him on the spot.

DEUTERONOMY, SCHMOOTERONOMY, LET'S CALL THE WHOLE THING OFF!

KELOWNA, BRITISH COLUMBIA

MOVE over road rage.

Move over road hogs, bumper-riders, careless lane-changers and cell phone operators.

Just when we thought we'd exhausted the list of the dumb, dangerous, and downright stupid things that have turned our highways into battle zones, along comes a pair of Sunday drivers hell-bent on settling religious differences as they barreled along the highway of life.

A 21-year-old Kelowna area man and his girl-friend were discussing religion while out for a Sunday drive when the disagreement took place.

Police say the difference of opinion, over a passage from the Bible, moved quickly from the spiritual arena to something more closely resembling a WWF special on wheels.

It was, the story has it, a simple case of his interpretation of the biblical passage versus hers, until all hell broke loose, and ended up in court where the young man apologized to his girlfriend for his abominable behavior.

Hallelujah and Amen!

I Knew Red Adair, and You, Sir, Are No Red Adair

PARIS

PARISIANS joined in a one-fingered salute to the drunken tourist who ended up in hospital after his futile attempt to extinguish their "eternal flame," with his ass.

Hospital officials said burns to the man's nether regions were superficial and would heal quickly.

Newspaper reports indicate the flame, which has been burning under the Arc de Triomphe since 1921, remained lit. The flame honours French soldiers killed during World War I.

Police say it is not the first time that the flame has been "the butt" of pranksters. During the 1998 World Cup, a drunken Mexican soccer fan attempted to put out the fire by pouring water on it. The previous year, an Australian was nabbed while attempting to boil an egg over it.

And While You're Here, How About Some Nice Oceanfront Property in Saskatchewan?

TORONTO

A knife-wielding bandit was apprehended after a quick thinking employee in a lingerie shop convinced him that his robbery was being recorded on the store's video surveillance camera and suggested that they shut it off immediately.

What the robber didn't know was that the young lady forgot to switch the camera on when she arrived at the store earlier that day.

"I asked him if he wanted me to shut it off," she told police, "and when he said 'yes,' well I just reached over and turned it on."

According to police, not only did the video camera provide "excellent footage" of the man's starring role in the mini-drama, but the plucky 30-year-old then followed him out of the store, took down his license number, and with the help of a passer-by who just happened to have a cell phone, alerted police.

"Stop, or I'll Shoot!"
"No, You Stop, or I'll Shoot!"

SEATTLE, WASHINGTON

THE O-K Corral visited downtown Seattle when three policemen got into a western-style shoot-em-up after mistaking each other's vehicles for a stolen squad car.

Fortunately, no one got hurt.

A police spokesperson said the confusion began when a bicycle patrol officer, certain that he had spotted a stolen police car, radioed in the mid-city location.

As one squad car sped into the area in hot pursuit it was spotted by another patrolman in another car who — assuming he had the thief or thieves in his sights — rammed the speeding cruiser from behind.

Convinced they were being attacked, the officers in the first car opened fire and the gunfight was underway.

The officers involved — two in one vehicle, one in the other — fired more than 20 rounds before they realized their error.

Now, Will You Believe Me?

CAPE TOWN, SOUTH AFRICA

UPSET by what he called a "crime wave" sweeping his country and a perceived lack of support for local police forces, a public spirited South African began a 4,000 kilometre trek to draw public attention to lawlessness and disorder.

Roger Russell guessed his marathon hike, from Cape Town to Johannesburg and back again, would take approximately six months to complete.

But alas, as police reported, the young do-gooder was mugged and robbed at gunpoint just 20 kilometres from his departure point on the second day of his expedition.

Police say the thieves escaped with everything except the clothes Russell was wearing at the time of the robbery.

Another Coffee, Marge?
No Thanks Herbie,
I'd Better Get Back To Work.

GLASGOW

AIRPORT officials grumbled, and angry relatives watched helplessly from the airport lounge as a flight carrying 55 passengers circled overhead for a full half hour while the terminal's only air traffic controller took a break for lunch.

Officials blamed the incident on a shortage of air traffic controllers, saying the one on duty that day had to take her break at that time because national aviation regulations do not allow a controller to work more than two hours without one.

Newscasts spoke of angry and exasperated families waiting in the little airport on the island of Benbecula as the flight from Glasgow hung about the sky, "tantalizingly within view."

Glory Be, and if it Isn't Bridget Murphy, and Lookin' Every Bit as Beautiful as the Day Itself

DUBLIN

NOT only can you not go home again, but if it's robbery you've got on your mind, then perhaps you shouldn't even think about it. Or, if you think about it at all, do make certain that your thoughts are sober ones.

For wasn't it a crock of John Barleycorn, and a Christmas visit to the neighbourhood of his youth that proved a fateful combination for 23-year-old Paul Fulham from the village of Drogheda.

Blame it on the excitement of the season, the happiness of seeing so many familiar faces, an alcoholic haze perhaps, or maybe even that green-green grass of home, but there he was in the middle of a hold-up, waving a knife while falling down drunk, and standing up and falling down again, and lifting his mask to shout hello and "Top o' the Season" to people he recognized.

So drunk was the lad that when the time came to flee the scene, he was unable to find the door, thereby displaying, according to his own lawyer, a total lack of "criminal professionalism."

DUMB MEN AND THE WOMEN WHO LOVE THEM

FOCSANI, ROMANIA

"A" is for ashtray.

"B" is for the back of the head.

"C" is for the clumsy Casanova who got an ashtray in the back of the noodle after giving his wife jewelry with his mistress's initials on it, and giving his mistress a gold and silver necklace with his wife's initials dangling from the clasp.

Police say the necklace mix-up triggered a domestic dustup that sent this romantic Romanian to hospital after he was knocked unconscious by a marble ashtray hurled his way by his very angry wife.

Police would not comment on the mistress's reaction to the necklace with the wife's initials, saying only that it probably spelled even more trouble for the alphabetically challenged chump.

PROSECUTOR NOT WORRIED ABOUT CONVICTION, SAYS IT'S IN THE BAG

ST. PETERSBURG, FLORIDA

A 35-year-old convenience store robber walked off with less than $100 but left an image on the store's security camera that police called extremely valuable, if not priceless.

Herbert Hill told police that he entered the store to rob the place when he suddenly realized that he had no nylon stocking, no balaclava, no disguise of any kind to hide his face, so he grabbed a clear plastic garbage bag and pulled it over his head.

As a disguise, the bag left a lot to be desired.

"He's like looking through this big prophylactic," said one policeman. "We got a real nice video."

I'm Sorry, This Is Not a Recording

TORONTO

WHEN he pulled her over for speeding, she was on her cellphone and the constable stood there, tapping his foot in the dirt at the side of the road, waiting patiently for her conversation to end.

When she finally finished chatting, she handed over her driver's license and ownership papers and the constable returned to his cruiser to write up a ticket.

When he walked back to deliver her speeding citation, damned if she wasn't on the phone again, and the constable waited even longer this time while the lady wrapped up yet another animated and lengthy conversation.

Back in his cruiser, the constable mulls the pros and cons of phones in cars, and is getting ready to ticket another speeder when WHAMMO! — his cruiser is suddenly rammed from behind.

According to the constable, he recognized her immediately as the lady he had just finished ticketing.

"I'm sorry," said the lady who had just rear-ended him. "I was on my cellphone, taking a message."

Now Here's a Little Number That Should Get You at Least Forty Winks to the Gallon

GRAND FALLS, NEW BRUNSWICK

COURT officials, newspaper editors, radio and television commentators all had something to smile about when police in this northern New Brunswick town suggested that a spell behind bars should give a 21-year-old local man an opportunity to consider a less exhausting line of work.

The charge — car napping.

"I guess stealing cars just plain wears him out," commented one officer, explaining that the young man was found sound asleep in a stolen vehicle — not once, but twice.

The first time he was arrested, the young sleepyhead was discovered snoring in the open trunk of a four-door sedan just boosted from a local car dealership.

Several weeks later, still awaiting a trial date on the first offence, police again arrested him — this time catching forty winks behind the wheel of a stolen pickup truck.

Said a court official at the young man's sentencing, "Two and a half years should give him plenty of time to consider a less tiring line of work."

That's Strange, It Worked When I Tried It... at Home

ACCRA

A 23-year-old Ghanaian was shot and killed while trying out a bulletproof potion concocted for him by a village witchdoctor.

According to the Ghana News Agency, the young man was one of 16 who had asked the local witchdoctor or *jujuman* to make them invulnerable to bullets, swords and arrows of neighbouring tribesmen.

After applying the herbal lotion to his body for several weeks, the man volunteered to test its effectiveness by having a friend shoot him with a rifle.

Villagers say the man died instantly.

No word on whether the witchdoctor will be tried for bad medicine.

Hello, 911?
I'd Like to Report a Law Firm
Totally Out of Control

SAN JOSE, CALIFORNIA

IN what appears to have been an all out attempt to prove they are as bright-eyed and clear-headed as the rest of the dummies in this book, a California law firm delivered 600 packages containing fake hand grenades to would-be clients.

Meant to suggest a "Business is War" message, the sales promotional gimmick backfired, sending shudders through the ranks of recipients, and prompting at least two Silicon Valley companies to call in the bomb squad.

The firm has since apologized to the companies on its mailing list.

Because the intent behind the mailing was not malicious, police say that the U.S. Postal Service will not pursue the matter.

Puzzled bomb squad officers are still shaking their heads over the marketing disaster.

"The guy that dreamed this one up will probably be selling refrigerators in Nome," commented one veteran of the response team.

Okay, Now Run Over Me With the Steam Roller and Throw Me Off That Cliff Over There...

SWAN RIVER, MANITOBA

YOU buy something new for yourself, you want to try it out, right?

Zip that BMW around the block.

Slap *The Dead* on the new sound system.

Pour a glass from that case of *Chateau Neuf de Papal Clemency.*

It's human nature.

At least that might explain the Swan River guy who came home from a trip to Alberta with a brand new bulletproof vest.

First off, he talks his best buddy into shooting him in the chest with a .22 calibre rifle and yep, you guessed it, the bullets bounced right off his chest like he was Superman.

Surviving that, the guy tucks a telephone book under the vest and talks his friend into shooting him again, this time with a 12-gauge shotgun.

The results — several cracked ribs, a whole lot of bruising, weapons charges against both men, one damaged phone book, and an admission by both that the shooting wasn't exactly the brightest thing they had ever done.

And Finally, What History of Mensa Would Be Complete Without a Word From These Two Guys

TORONTO

POLICE won't release the name of the truck driver who used his cigarette lighter to see if he had completely drained the contents of his tanker truck. "He's probably embarrassed enough," says one officer, explaining that the man had just delivered a load of highly flammable liquids when the accident occurred.

The man told police he used his lighter because his flashlight was broken and ...

WHOOOOSH!

A single flick and there go the eyebrows, and there goes the beard, and there goes the careless trucker, tossed four metres by the resulting explosion.

"My guess is he'll use a razor next time he wants a shave that close," said a lady police officer at the scene.

LITTLE ROCK, ARKANSAS

MEANWHILE, down in Little Rock, J. M. Tomplins wondered whether that was gas or water in his jerrycan, reached down for his trusty Zippo lighter and ...

But you know the story.

Not the Handiest Gadget in the Toolbox?

A Few Peas Shy of a Casserole?

Not the Brightest Bulb in the Marquee?

*A Flash of Light, A Cloud of Dust,
And ... What Was the Question?*

IF you have a story you would like to see included in a future edition of this book, please send a newspaper clipping, or a transcript of the radio or television newscast on which the story aired to,

Three Bricks
c/o Fitzhenry & Whiteside
195 Allstate Parkway
Markham, Ontario L3R 4T8

Or
godwit@fitzhenry.ca

If your story is chosen, you will receive a complimentary copy of the next collection. Where two or more people have submitted the same story, the publisher will send a complimentary book to the individual whose story was received first.

*All submissions must be accompanied by the name and address of the newspaper from which the story has been clipped, or the name and address of the radio or television station on which it was heard.